MONTVILLE TWP. PUBLIC LIBRARY
90 HORSENECK ROAD
MONTVILLE, N.J. 07045

090163²

P9-BZT-227
0 1021 0238050 2

Snap books™

Queens and Princesses

Marie Antoinette

QUEEN OF FRANCE

by Mary Englar

Consultant:

Tifenn Judet de la Combe

The French Library and Cultural Center

Boston, Massachusetts

Capstone press®

Mankato, Minnesota

Snap Books are published by Capstone Press,
151 Good Counsel Drive, P.O. Box 669, Mankato, Minnesota 56002.
www.capstonepress.com

Copyright © 2009 by Capstone Press, a Capstone Publishers company.
All rights reserved. No part of this publication may be reproduced in whole or in
part, or stored in a retrieval system, or transmitted in any form or by any means,
electronic, mechanical, photocopying, recording, or otherwise, without written
permission of the publisher. For information regarding permission, write to Capstone
Press, 151 Good Counsel Drive, P.O. Box 669, Dept. R, Mankato, Minnesota 56002.
Printed in the United States of America

Library of Congress Cataloging-in-Publication Data
Englar, Mary.
    Marie Antoinette, queen of France / by Mary Englar.
    p. cm. — (Snap books. Queens and princesses)
    Summary: "Describes the life and death of Queen Marie Antoinette of France" —
Provided by publisher.
    Includes bibliographical references and index.
    ISBN-13: 978-1-4296-1956-1 (hardcover)
    ISBN-10: 1-4296-1956-2 (hardcover)
    1. Marie Antoinette, Queen, consort of Louis XVI, King of France, 1755–1793 —
Juvenile literature. 2. Queens — France — Biography — Juvenile literature.
3. France — History — Louis XVI, 1774–1793 — Juvenile literature. I. Title.
II. Series.
DC137.1.E54 2009
944'.035092 — dc22   2008007550

Editor: Angie Kaelberer
Designer: Juliette Peters
Photo Researcher: Wanda Winch

Photo Credits: Art Resource, N.Y./ Réunion des Musées Nationaux, 11; The
Bridgeman Art Library International/Schloss Schonbrunn, Vienna, Austria/
Archduchess Marie Antoinette Habsburg-Lotharingen (1755–93) 1767–68 (oil on
canvas), Mytens or Meytens, Martin II (1695–1770), 12; Getty Images Inc./The
Bridgeman Art Library, 17; Getty Images Inc./The Bridgeman Art Library/Josef
Hauzinger, 21; Getty Images Inc./Hulton Archive, 25; Getty Images Inc./Hulton
Archive/Imagno, 9, 15, 16, 18; Getty Images Inc./National Geographic/James L.
Stanfield, 26; Getty Images Inc./Roger Viollet/ND, 5; The Image Works/Heritage-
Images/Art Media, 6; The Image Works/Roger-Viollet, 22; Library of Congress, 29;
SuperStock Inc./Christie's Images, cover

Essential content terms are bold and are defined at the bottom of the page where
they first appear.

1 2 3 4 5 6 13 12 11 10 09 08

0 1021 0238050 2

Table of Contents

02/2009
CAP
$ 17.99

ROYAL *Wedding* DAY

On the morning of May 16, 1770, Marie Antoinette arrived by carriage at the palace of Versailles near Paris, France. That afternoon, she would marry the **dauphin** of France, Louis Auguste. He was the grandson of King Louis XV.

French noblemen and women crowded at the palace windows. Everyone hoped to catch a glimpse of the bride. Those who saw her were impressed. Marie Antoinette's ash blond hair was thick and shiny. She had beautiful pale skin and blue eyes.

At age 14, Marie Antoinette traveled to France to marry a boy she had never even met.

dauphin — the male next in line to be the king of France

Marie Antoinette stared at the palace. Versailles was even larger than the palaces she had lived in. Marie Antoinette was only 14, and she had just met 15-year-old Louis Auguste two days before. Except for servants, she traveled alone from her home in Vienna, Austria. None of her family had made the trip.

A CELEBRATION TO REMEMBER

Marie Antoinette's servants rushed her into the palace to get ready for the wedding. In her rooms, she found many expensive gifts. King Louis XV gave her a large red velvet chest filled with presents. Each silk-lined drawer held a collar of pearls, a diamond necklace, or bracelets with her initials.

Louis Auguste was only 15 when he met and married Marie Antoinette.

The servants dressed Marie Antoinette in a silver, gold, and rose brocade gown. The silk gown fit tight around her upper body. It flowed over the large hoops beneath her skirt into a long train.

Gracefully, Marie Antoinette walked through the palace's Hall of Mirrors with Louis Auguste at her side. King Louis XV and other family members and friends followed them. After they entered the Royal Chapel, the young couple knelt down to say their wedding vows. Louis Auguste's hand shook as he placed the ring on Marie Antoinette's finger.

The wedding celebration went on long into the night. Marie Antoinette was surrounded by 6,000 guests dressed in their best silk coats and gowns. Lanterns lit the gardens as the guests danced. Fireworks exploded over the palace after dark.

When the party was over, the high-ranking nobles followed the couple into Louis Auguste's rooms. After a priest blessed their bed, the king helped Louis Auguste into bed. Then, a duchess helped Marie Antoinette get into bed. Those in the room bowed or curtsied before they left. For the first time, the two teenagers were alone. After all the excitement of the day, Marie Antoinette finally had time to miss her home and family in Austria.

Antoine of Austria

On November 2, 1755, a little **archduchess** was born to Emperor Francis Stephen and Empress Maria Theresa of Austria. The emperor and empress named the baby Maria Antonia Josepha Joanna. They called her Antonia or Antoine for short.

Today, a family with five or six children is considered large. But Antoine had 15 brothers and sisters! She was the 15th child and the 11th daughter. Three of her older sisters had died when they were babies or small children.

Antoine's parents were faithful members of the Roman Catholic Church. All of the girls' names began with Maria, to honor the Virgin Mary. Antoine was close to her sister, Maria Caroline, who was three years older. Maria Caroline was called Charlotte.

Antoine came from a very large family. This portrait was painted before her birth in 1755.

archduchess — an Austrian princess

FAMILY LIFE IN VIENNA

Antoine's family lived in two palaces each year. In winter, they lived in Vienna in the Hofburg Palace. In spring and summer, the family lived in the Schönbrunn Palace. This palace was about 5 miles (8 kilometers) from Vienna.

Antoine and Charlotte loved the Schönbrunn. They each had five rooms in their apartments. The girls played together in the gardens every day. They watched the camel, the rhinoceros, the mountain lion, and the colorful parrots at the palace zoo.

During winter, the children took swan-shaped sleighs out for a ride. Antoine and her sisters dressed in velvet coats trimmed with fur and diamonds. Antoine loved the nighttime sleigh rides by torchlight.

AN ARCHDUCHESS' EDUCATION

Antoine's parents ruled the Holy Roman Empire, which included the countries of Austria, Hungary, and Bohemia. Antoine's mother handled all of the business of the empire. She had little time to spend with her many children. Antoine's father enjoyed hunting more than work. He was cheerful and caring with Antoine and her siblings.

A **governess** taught Antoine her school lessons. Antoine loved her kind governess, who often covered up for Antoine when she didn't know her lessons. Antoine was a dreamer. She disliked reading, and writing took too much time. She often made mistakes.

When Antoine was 11, her mother discovered that Antoine barely knew how to write. Also, she read very slowly. The empress hired a strict new governess for Antoine to improve her skills. Antoine wanted to please her mother. She feared reading lessons because she failed so often.

Antoine loved to dance. At age 9, she performed a dance at the wedding of her older brother Joseph II.

FAMILY TRAGEDIES

In August 1765, Antoine's father died suddenly of a stroke. Two years later, **smallpox** struck the family. Two of Antoine's older sisters caught the disease. Maria Josepha died at age 16. Maria Elizabeth, who was 23, was left with terrible scars.

Antoine's mother had arranged marriages for both girls before they got sick. Josepha was supposed to marry King Ferdinand of Naples. Instead, Charlotte was sent in her place. Antoine cried when her favorite sister left for Italy. Elizabeth's marriage was called off because of her scars.

By the time Antoine was 13, her mother was preparing her for marriage.

smallpox — a deadly disease

Antoine and her sisters always knew they would marry strangers. Their arranged marriages improved relationships with other European countries. Maria Theresa wanted Antoine to marry French royalty. France and Austria were often at war, but a royal marriage would help their relationship.

Maria Theresa wanted Antoine to look her best. She had a dentist straighten Antoine's teeth. Antoine spent three months in the metal wires. Maria Theresa also worried about Antoine's high forehead. A hairdresser fixed Antoine's hair so her forehead didn't show. Then an artist painted Antoine's portrait.

Maria Theresa sent Antoine's portrait to King Louis XV in 1769. She asked that the king consider pretty Antoine for his grandson, Louis Auguste. King Louis agreed, and the teenagers became engaged. No one asked Antoine or Louis Auguste how they felt about the marriage.

"I love the empress but I'm frightened of her. Even at a distance, when I'm writing to her, I never feel completely at ease."

Marie Antoinette writing about her mother

Queen of France

When Antoine married Louis Auguste, she became the new **dauphine** of France. In French, her name became Marie Antoinette. Her most important job would be to give birth to a son who would one day be king.

Marie Antoinette had to learn the customs of the French royal court. These rules were known as L'Etiquette. A noblewoman named Madame de Noailles was in charge of teaching Marie Antoinette about L'Etiquette. The dauphine soon got tired of constantly being corrected.

In April 1774, King Louis XV caught smallpox and died. Suddenly, Louis Auguste and Marie Antoinette were the new king and queen of France. Louis Auguste became King Louis XVI. He was 19, and Marie Antoinette was just 18.

> Marie Antoinette felt unprepared for her new role as queen of France.

dauphine — the wife of the future king of France

The queen hosted parties where she played the harp and sang for her friends.

LIFE AS A QUEEN

Marie Antoinette had 500 servants waiting on her. Her servants woke her up, dressed her, and fixed her hair. Each servant had a different responsibility.

The queen did not like all the attention, but she loved choosing new clothes and jewelry. Three large rooms filled with dresses, shoes, and jewelry made up the queen's wardrobe. Every day, the Mistress of the Robes brought Marie Antoinette the wardrobe book. This book included pictures and material samples from each of her outfits. The queen used a pin to mark her choices for that day. She wore riding outfits for hunting, new dresses at every ball, and casual cotton dresses in the garden.

FRIENDS AT THE COURT

Marie Antoinette made friends with the young noblewomen of France. Many of them were relatives of the king. The queen and her friends went to the opera and the theater. They played cards far into the night. The queen enjoyed playing the harp and singing for her friends.

In 1774, King Louis gave his wife a small château on the palace grounds. The house was called Petit Trianon. Marie Antoinette decorated Petit Trianon in soft shades of blue and green. She filled it with roses and hosted elegant parties there. She and her friends acted in plays in the château's private theater.

THE POUF

After being dressed for the day, Marie Antoinette had her hair done. Her hairdresser started with a wire form 3 feet (1 meter) high. He wrapped her hair around the form and added fake hair to fill in the form. When finished, the hairdresser dusted powder on her hair and added decorations. The queen was famous for her creative hair ornaments, including vegetables and toy boats. Every lady at the court watched to see the queen's fashionable poufs.

Marie Antoinette lived more than 600 miles (965 kilometers) away from her family. But her mother still had much influence on her. Maria Theresa wrote long letters to her daughter about how to be a good wife and a good queen.

Marie Antoinette believed her husband had little interest in her. He spent his days hunting. The empress warned her daughter that she must produce a son to save her marriage. She also encouraged Marie Antoinette to use her power as queen to help Austria, her home country. The empress wanted France on Austria's side.

This portrait originally included all four of Marie Antoinette's children. Baby Sophie was painted out after her death in 1787.

> "At noon, all the world can enter . . . I put on
> my rouge and wash my hands before everybody."
>
> Marie Antoinette in a letter to her mother, 1770

A FAMILY AT LAST

At age 23, Marie Antoinette finally had a child in December 1778. The king and all his relatives were in the room during the birth of the baby girl. After the birth, Marie Antoinette passed out from the heat and lack of air in the stuffy room. The baby was named Marie Thérèse-Charlotte. She was known as Madame Royale.

In late 1780, the queen received a message from Vienna. Maria Theresa had died the week before. Marie Antoinette was heartbroken that she would never see her mother again.

Nearly a year later, Marie Antoinette had a second child. This time, she allowed only her closest friends and the king in her bedroom. When the baby was born, everyone was silent. The queen feared that the baby was a girl. King Louis finally told her that she'd given birth to the next king of France. The king and queen named the baby Louis Joseph.

Marie Antoinette was happy to be a mother. She loved her children and hoped for more. In 1785, she had a second son, Louis Charles. He was followed by another girl in 1786, Sophie Hélène Béatrice. Sophie was not healthy, and she died a year later. The queen grieved over the loss of her youngest child.

The queen wanted her children to have a better education than she had received. She paid close attention to their lessons and made sure they were making progress.

Revolution
IN THE AIR

The queen and king lived nearly all of their lives at Versailles. They had everything they wanted. They never saw how the French people lived in the countryside.

The **peasants** of France worked hard on their farms. They ate what they grew on the farms. If their crops died, they had no money for food. They owed taxes even when their crops failed. They paid a tax to the king and to the Catholic Church. They also gave part of their crop to the landowner. In contrast, the wealthy people usually paid much less in taxes than the peasants did.

During Marie Antoinette's years at Versailles, France went through several droughts and a very cold winter. The peasants were desperate for food. The king knew of these disasters, but he couldn't change the tax laws to make them fairer. The regional parliaments had to agree to new taxes. The parliaments were made up of nobles and landowners who didn't want to pay more taxes.

Louis (center) and Marie Antoinette did their best to rule France, but many people were unhappy with them.

peasant — a person who worked on or owned a small farm

CUTTING BACK

The king and queen tried to cut costs. Marie Antoinette let 173 servants go and ordered fewer dresses. The king gave up some of his horses. The French people were still angry about the unfair taxes. They especially blamed Marie Antoinette for spending money on clothing, fine furniture, and jewelry.

But the queen's expenses were only part of the problem. France had spent huge amounts fighting the Seven Years' War (1756–1763). The country also helped the American colonies win their war of independence against Great Britain. These wars left France with no money to help its people.

In October 1789, a huge crowd of women marched to Versailles.

A VIOLENT SUMMER

Marie Antoinette's oldest son, Louis Joseph, had been sick with tuberculosis for several years. By the spring of 1789, his parents knew he was dying. Marie Antoinette took the 7-year-old boy to the countryside. She hoped the fresh air would help him, but he died in June.

While the king and queen mourned their son at Versailles, the people of France started a revolution. They formed a new government. In July 1789, the rebels attacked the Bastille prison in Paris. Large amounts of weapons and gunpowder were stored at the prison. The rebels planned to use the weapons to fight the king's army.

In October, about 6,000 women marched from Paris to Versailles. They demanded bread for their families. A mob of angry citizens formed around the women. At 4:00 in the morning, the mob attacked the palace guards.

Marie Antoinette ran down a secret hallway to the king's rooms. The terrified king and queen behaved calmly for their children's sake. The crowd outside called for Marie Antoinette and Louis to appear on the balcony. When they stepped out, the crowd demanded they go to Paris.

Louis knew they were not safe at Versailles. He hoped that his guards might have more control in Paris. It took the family hours to get to Paris. Their carriage pushed slowly through the angry mob. Marie Antoinette feared what would happen when they reached Paris.

A Tragic END

Marie Antoinette and her family were now prisoners of the new government. They were held in a castle called Les Tuileries. The French people argued over whether the king and his family should live. Some wanted to keep the royal family but reduce their power. Others argued that they should all be killed. These people wanted to build a republic, like the new United States.

A DARING ESCAPE

Louis and Marie Antoinette were worried about what would happen to their family. In the early morning hours of June 21, 1791, the family slipped away from their guards. They disguised themselves and fled Paris in a carriage. They were headed to Montmédy, a city about 270 miles (435 kilometers) from Paris. A loyal general was there with his army. This army was ready to protect the king and his family.

Marie Antoinette, Louis, and their two remaining children (left) were prisoners of the French government.

The family traveled all that day. About 11:00 that night, they reached Varennes. This town was about 150 miles (240 kilometers) from Paris. There, townspeople recognized the family and took them prisoner. The next morning, government officials arrived to bring the family back to Paris. The unsuccessful escape made the French people even angrier at the king and queen.

THE END

The family spent the next two years under constant guard. In August 1792, they were moved to a tower in Paris called the Temple. There they lived quietly. The king and queen taught their children their lessons. Once each day, the family went outside under the watchful eyes of the guards.

In January 1793, King Louis said good-bye to Marie Antoinette and the children for the last time.

In December 1792, the new government put Louis on trial for treason and other crimes against France. He was found guilty and was put to death on January 21, 1793. In July, Louis Charles was taken from his mother to a different part of the Temple. A month later, guards moved Marie Antoinette to another jail. She never saw either of her children again.

THE DIAMOND NECKLACE AFFAIR

Even something as small as a piece of jewelry caused problems for Marie Antoinette. In 1781, two Paris jewelers tried to sell the queen a necklace of 647 glittering diamonds. The queen was trying to cut back on spending and said no.

A dishonest woman named Jeanne de la Motte then got involved. In 1784, de la Motte went to Cardinal de Rohan, the French bishop. She told the cardinal she was a close friend of the queen's. She said the queen wanted the necklace, but didn't want the king to know she had bought it. De Rohan wanted to be on good terms with the queen. He agreed to buy the necklace in secret. He didn't know that Marie Antoinette had never even met Jeanne de la Motte.

De Rohan gave the necklace to de la Motte, telling her to give it to the queen. Instead, she broke the necklace apart and sold the stones separately. When de Rohan asked the queen to pay for the necklace, he learned she knew nothing about it. Both de Rohan and de la Motte were arrested. De Rohan was found not guilty, while de la Motte was sentenced to prison.

Many French people believed the queen had worked with de la Motte to ruin Cardinal de Rohan's reputation. The Diamond Necklace Affair gave them one more reason to hate their queen.

On October 16, 1793, Marie Antoinette was found guilty of treason. Later that day, she was put to death. She was only 37 years old.

As Marie Antoinette waited for her execution, she wrote a letter to the king's sister Elisabeth. She asked Elisabeth to take care of her children. Ten-year-old Louis Charles died in prison in June 1795. Six months later, Madame Royale was released and sent to Austria. She died in 1851 at age 73.

For years, people blamed Marie Antoinette for the French Revolution. Today, most historians believe that Marie Antoinette was no worse than the queens before her. For 37 years, she lived as she had been raised. From archduchess to queen, she lived in a separate world from ordinary people.

LET THEM EAT CAKE!

Many French people disliked Marie Antoinette from the day she arrived. France and Austria had long been enemies, and the French people did not trust the new queen. A false story spread that Marie Antoinette said, "Let them eat cake!" when she heard that the peasants had no bread. This meant that she did not care if they were starving, because cake cost more than bread. This myth is still repeated today, even though historians believe Marie Antoinette never said those words.

Guards took Marie Antoinette to her execution after her sentencing on October 16, 1793.

29

Glossary

archduchess (arch-DUH-chuss) — an Austrian princess

château (sha-TOW) — a large country house

dauphin (DO-fan) — the male next in line to be the king of France

dauphine (DO-feen) — the wife of the future king of France

governess (GUH-vur-nuss) — a woman who cares for and teaches children in their home

peasant (PEZ-uhnt) — a person in Europe who worked on a farm or owned a small farm

revolution (rev-uh-LOO-shun) — an uprising by a group of people against a system of government or a way of life

smallpox (SMAWL-poks) — a disease that spreads easily from person to person, causing chills, fever, and pimples that scar; smallpox often causes death.

treason (TREE-zuhn) — the act of betraying one's country

tuberculosis (tu-BUR-kyoo-low-sis) — a disease caused by bacteria that causes fever, weight loss, and coughing; left untreated, tuberculosis can lead to death.

Read More

Barber, Nicola. *The French Revolution.* Questioning History. North Mankato, Minn.: Smart Apple Media, 2005.

Bingham, Jane. *Marie Antoinette.* Great Women Leaders. Chicago: Raintree, 2008.

Stewart, Gail B. *The French Revolution.* People at the Center of. Detroit: Thomson Gale, 2006.

Tagliaferro, Linda. *Palace of Versailles: France's Royal Jewel.* Castles, Palaces, and Tombs. New York: Bearport, 2005.

Internet Sites

FactHound offers a safe, fun way to find Internet sites related to this book. All of the sites on FactHound have been researched by our staff.

Here's how:

1. Visit *www.facthound.com*
2. Choose your grade level.
3. Type in this book ID **1429619562** for age-appropriate sites. You may also browse subjects by clicking on letters, or by clicking on pictures and words.
4. Click on the **Fetch It** button.

FactHound will fetch the best sites for you!

Index